A Quick and Easy Guide for Genealogists

Researching Your Ancestors Using the U.S. Census

Stephanie Pitcher Fishman

RHB

Rebecca Hills
Books

Researching Your Ancestors Using the U.S. Census by Stephanie Pitcher Fishman

Published by Rebecca Hills Books
Part of the Quick & Easy Guides for Genealogists series

Cover graphics from Pixabay.com under the Creative Commons license.

Thank you for purchasing this Quick & Easy Guide for Genealogists. Please consider leaving a review on the page that you purchased this book. By reviewing it and telling others, you will help me share this work with other family historians. I greatly appreciate your support!

Please visit the author's website at www.stephaniefishman.com.

Also by Stephanie Pitcher Fishman:
Finding Eliza
The Widow Teal

The Quick & Easy Genealogy Series:
Researching Your Quaker Family History
Researching the Plain Religions
Family Story Toolkit

For our ancestors, whether American by birth or American by choice.

Contents

Introduction

C ensus records are perhaps the first public record most genealogists use beyond vital records. Federal and state census records can provide valuable information on our ancestors as they record a variety of personal information including: head of household, address, number of children living, place of birth of the individual, place of birth of the parents, occupation, value of real and personal property, educational level, names of neighbors, and more.

Beginning in 1790, the United States federal government began enumerating the population every ten years. By analyzing the information provided on census schedules we can learn more about our ancestors' daily lives. Using simple tips and tricks you can put this record set securely in your tool belt.

Get ready to dig into U.S. Census records!

Basic Census Facts

F rom occupational information to marital status, census records provide a variety of information to help move our research ahead. Let's get started with some basic foundations of census research.

Dates of Availability

Existing US Federal Census records are available for the years 1790 to 1940. Due to privacy issues, census records are kept confidential for 72 years.

Future records will be made available on the following schedule:

- 1950: Available 2022
- 1960: Available 2032
- 1970: Available 2042
- 1980: Available 2052
- 1990: Available 2062
- 2000: Available 2072

Repository

The complete US Federal Census 1790-1940 with exception of the damaged 1890 census is held by the following repositories:

National Archives

Washington, DC and thirteen regional facilities

http://www.nara.gov

The Family History Library

Salt Lake City, Utah

http://www.familysearch.org

Allen County Public Library Genealogy Center

Fort Wayne, Indiana

http://genealogycenter.org

Access points

You may be able to find partial records, transcriptions, or other notes available on other websites. Many of these are listed in the Toolkit section of this guide. However, the sites listed below will be your main access points for your census record searches.

- Ancestry.com: http://www.ancestry.com
- FamilySearch: http://www.familysearch.org
- Archives.com: http://www.archives.com
- HeritageQuest:
  http://www.heritagequest.com
- 1940 Census:
  http://1940census.archives.gov/index.asp

Missing Records

The 1890 US Federal Census was destroyed by fire in 1921. Only partial records remain and indexes available have been constructed using additional extant records.

Substitute records for the 1890 US Federal Census include:

- Tax Lists
- Voter Registration Lists
- City Directories
- State Censuses
- 1890 Veterans Schedule
- Native American Tribal Census

Ancestry.com has a searchable 1890 Census Substitute database containing these and other record sets. You can find that here: http://ancstry.me/1S7UfKq

The 1790 US Federal Census records sustained damage during the War of 1812. Records for the following states were destroyed: Delaware, Kentucky, Georgia, New Jersey, Tennessee, and Virginia.

Additional records for enumeration districts, neighborhoods, or other areas may have sustained damage due to fire, flood, or simple loss. Your ancestor may have been enumerated even if you are not able to locate them in a state or federal census record.

The Federal Census Year by Year

1790

Census day: 2 August

The results of the 1790 US Federal Census were compiled into a series of books titled, *Heads of Families at the First Census of the United States*. Various volumes are available to read as ebooks on Google

Books. (books.google.com)

1800

Census Day: 4 August

The questions asked in the 1810 US Federal Census are identical to those asked in 1810.

1810

Census Day: 6 August

The questions asked in the 1810 US Federal Census are identical to those asked in 1800.

1820

Census Day: 7 August

Check the number of household members

carefully. Males and females may be counted twice as age division overlaps. This census also includes additional information on foreigners not naturalized, those involved in manufacturing and commerce, and in agriculture.

1830

Census Day: 1 June

The first uniform worksheets are used in this census year. Information is collected on individuals who are considered deaf, dumb, and blind, as well as on foreigners not naturalized.

1840

Census Day: 1 June

Revolutionary War pensioners are listed with

their current age. Results were compiled into a publication titled, *A Census of Pensioners for Revolutionary Or Military Services: with Their Names, Ages, and Places of Residence.* This is available to read as an ebook on Google Books. (books.google.com)

1850

Census Day: 1 June

This is the first census year to include the first names of all household members. Other identifying information recorded includes age, place of birth, occupation, value of real estate, if married within the year, education indicators, and if the individual is deaf, dumb, blind, insane, idiotic, pauper, or convict. Slave schedules were also used in southern states and New Jersey.

1860

Census Day: 1 June

In addition to those questions asked in 1850, the value of personal estate is also recorded. Slave schedules were also used in southern states and New Jersey.

1870

Census Day: 1 June

New questions on the 1870 census schedule include whether or not the enumerated individual's parents were of foreign birth and if the individual holds or was denied the right to vote.

1880

Census Day: 1 June

The 1880 census schedule is the first to include relationship to the head of household. Marital status is included in the vital statistics of the individual. Enumerators recorded the place of birth for the individual and their parents as well.

1890

Census Day: 1 June

A very limited amount of returns remain from the 1890 census. States with a portion surviving include: Alabama, Georgia, Illinois, Minnesota, New Jersey, New York, North Carolina, Ohio, South Dakota, and Texas. The remaining fragments are available for searching on Ancestry.com. (see "Substitute Records for the 1890 US Federal Census.")

1900

Census Day: 1 June

This census schedule is the only schedule to include both month and year of birth. House number and street are recorded on the worksheet for each household. Women are asked the number of living children as well as the total number of children born. This is useful for calculating children who could have died between census years. Year of immigration and naturalization status are also included.

1910

Census Day: 15 April

Additional occupational information is available including the number of weeks the individual may have been out of work in 1909. Union and Confederate veterans are enumerated on this census schedule.

1920

Census Day: 1 January

The 1920 US Federal Census schedule is the only schedule to ask the year of naturalization which is very helpful for researching your immigrant ancestors who were enumerated at this time. "Mother Tongue" is recorded for the individual and their parents in addition to country of birth.

1930

Census Day: 1 April (1 October for Alaska)

Citizenship and veterans status is again included in the 1930 US Federal Census schedule. Additional fun questions include if the family owned a radio set. Farms are listed along with their number on the farm schedule.

1940

Census Day: 1 April

The newly released 1940 US Federal Census supplies a greater amount of social statistics and information than previous census schedules. Note that the individual with an X is the person within the household that supplied the information. Residence is also listed for 1935 which allows researchers to place their ancestors on the map between census years. Additional occupational and educational information in include.

Something fun to note is that two individuals from each page are asked additional supplementary questions that provide information on military history, social security participation, and more. If you are lucky enough to have a relative in this situation you can have a unique peek into their lives.

Tips & Tricks

C ensus records can give you a wealth of information about your ancestors. Here are some of my favorite tips and tricks to squeezing the last drop of knowledge out of each enumerator's notations so that you can form the best picture available of your family.

Create a Person

Sometimes the best way to find a hole in our

research - or to fill one - is to tell a story. With each census, write the information in narrative form. Add each narrative to the last to create a picture of the person's life. By looking at it in story form rather than on the worksheet may allow you to see additional areas for further research. It will also allow you to visual the individual as a whole person rather than just a statistic.

Missing Families

Until 1870, only free, tax-paying males and their households were enumerated. If your ancestor is missing this could be why! Take a look at what category your ancestor would fall into compared to what was enumerated to see if they could have been in the home but not recorded. In this case, alternate records will need to be found.

Double Entries

It's possible for individuals to appear in the census multiple times. Depending on the census year, the enumerators were given a period between one and eighteen months to complete the enumeration. Families could have moved or traveled to see relatives. If you have a household that migrated during a census year, check the previous enumeration district for another entry that may contain additional information.

Look at the Location

The 1900 and 1910 US Federal Census procedures instructed enumerators to list an individual's birthplace by the current name or region rather than the name it used at the time of birth.

This could mean that a birth state is listed as West Virginia when it was actually Virginia at the time of birth. Consult period maps for clarification before making your game plan for future research.

Migration Patterns

Missing your family? If your ancestors migrated often, track their census locations on a blank map of the United States. Compare this to known migration routes for religious groups, time periods, events such as the Gold Rush, etc. to locate them in missing census years.

Neighborhood Analysis

To get a better idea of the social conditions surrounding your family, take note of the households around them. In addition to looking at the names of neighbors for possible relatives, note their occupation, real and personal estate values, educational levels, etc.

What does this tell you about their area? Was it a factory town? Was education important in their area, or did most children leave school at a young age? Analyzing those around our ancestors can help us to understand their daily lives in more detail.

Time Line Analysis

Create a time line listing each individual in your chosen household. Note the location where each person appeared during each census year. This has helped me not only identify what I've missed in my research but also interesting information such as the migration pattern that I may need to follow.

To see the effect of events such as the Civil War or World War I on your family, note the conditions recorded in the census year prior to the war as well as the census year after.

Analyze Relationships

Stepchildren or adopted children are not clearly marked in the census records. Also, do not assume that a boarder is (or is not) a relative. Either case could be true.

Rule of Three

Don't stop at the census sheet that enumerates your ancestor. Look at the sheet before and after for any related surnames - three sheets in total for each family. Keep a list of neighbor surnames for later in case it is needed for later analysis. Often, neighbors are friends and relatives that can help establish relationships in the case of a difficult brick wall.

Working with
Pre-1850 Census Records

Translate your household from names to "dashes and slashes." Using the age divisions provided within each pre-1850 census year, create a master showing the possible age groupings for your household. Remember to use all variations in cases where one person may be listed twice. If the birth date is known, compare it to the census enumeration date to determine the correct age for the individual when assigning them to a column.

Rather than looking for just the surname of your family, look for the combination of "dashes and slashes" on the schedule.

Special Search of Census Records: "Age Search"

The US Census Bureau will perform a requested search of confidential census years (1950 to present) for a named person if you are: the named person, the heir, or the legal guardian. If the individual is deceased, you will need to provide a death certificate with proof of the applicant as beneficiary or legal representative. There is a significant fee for this service. More information can be found at: http://1.usa.gov/1RzAfQ3

Special Circumstances

C ensus record are easy to locate and read if you have a male ancestor who has a complete name, spelled correctly, enumerated in the area that you expected, with a complete nuclear family represented. But what if you have a special circumstance? These tips will help.

Women and the Census

Women were, at times, listed by nicknames when

enumerated. Become familiar with typical nicknames and abbreviations for female names. When a woman's middle name is included, consider if this could possibly be a maiden name. Also, an elderly woman living in the home may be a boarder or she could be the mother in law of the head of household.

Remember that relationships are not always clearly or correctly defined. Although wives are not listed by name in census records prior to 1850, a woman would be listed if she were a widow.

Also note that if her husband perished in a war or conflict as part of the Union Army or Navy, a woman may be listed on the 1890 Special Union Veterans and Widows schedule.

Veterans and the Census

Key years for military research data in the census include:

- 1840: Revolutionary War pensioners
- 1890: Civil War veterans; additional Special Union Veterans and Widows Schedule
- 1910: Union Navy or Army; Confederate Navy or Army
- 1930: Civil War, Spanish-American War, Philippine Insurrection, Boxer Rebellion, Mexican Expedition, or World War.

Slaves and the Census

Slaves were reported in a separate schedule for only two census years: 1850 and 1860. Prior to 1850, enslaved individuals were listed by statistic only alongside their owner. The Slave Schedules of 1850 and 1860 did not list the individuals by name, though they did indicate age and sex which could prove helpful in identifying them when paired with additional record sets. If the slave died between 1849-1850 or 1859-1860 they may be enumerated in the appropriate Mortality Schedule. If the individual was alive in 1870, they would be enumerated by name for the first time.

State Census Records

State census records can help supply information about our ancestors between federal census years, specifically during the period of 1880 to 1900 when the 1890 US Federal Census is missing.

State archives, historical societies, and Libraries

should be consulted for the location of each state's census record collections. Both Ancestry.com and FamilySearch hold partial collections of various state census records. Consult their on line catalog for complete holdings.

Look for local censuses taken by county of tax payers, registered voters, members of militia, and more.

Non-Population Schedules

Agricultural Schedule: A special census enumerating the holdings of individual farms was taken in the years 1840 -1910. This typically included the owner's name, farm location, assets, animals raised or crops grown, etc.

Defective, Dependent, and Delinquent Classes Schedule: A special census was taken only in 1880 to enumerate the following groups: insane inhabitants of institutions, those with extreme mental deficiency (termed idiots), deaf-mutes, the blind or semi-blind, homeless children in institutions, those imprisoned in a prison or jail, and those in poorhouses or institutions. An individual could appear in multiple supplemental schedules within this schedule.

Manufacturing Schedule: A special census enumerating the statistics of manufacturing and industry was taken from 1810-1880. This scheduled included information such as the location of business, machinery owned, capital invested, etc. The Manufacturing Schedule was also called the Industry Schedule from 1850-1870. The 1870 schedule differentiates between the child and adult worker.

Mortality Schedule: A special census schedule was taken from 1850-1885 for the purpose of enumerating individuals who died during the 12 months preceding the census.

Social Statistics Schedule: This special census schedule was used to gather statistics on income, public debt, taxes, schools, libraries, newspapers, churches, those incarcerated, and more. This schedule was taken from 1850 through 1870 and again in 1885.

Veterans Schedule: A special census enumerating veterans from the Revolutionary and Civil Wars. Veterans Schedules were taken from 1840 to 1890.

The 1890 Veterans Schedule may be used to help fill in the gap created by the loss of the 1890 US Federal Census.

Transcription Tips

L ike with other record sets, you will want to either print or download copies of the census sheet on which your ancestor appears. This digital copy is great; however, a transcription of the record will help you pull every bit of information from it as well as will allow you to spot inconsistencies or missing facts.

Here are a few basic tips that will help you get the most out of your transcriptions.

1. If the handwriting of the enumerator is

difficult to read, here are some tips that might help, create a "cheat sheet" by tracing known letters from other names on this or additional pages.

2. When transcribing a census record onto a blank worksheet always write the entry exactly as it appears. If a name or location is crossed out or abbreviated transcribe it in the same manner on your blank worksheet. Clues may be lost within your translation of the enumerator's entry.

3. Although enumerators were given specific instructions for completing the census schedules, some would include their own notes. Be sure to look at the margins of the page for any notation, even those that appear to be stray marks. Include these in your transcription for later analysis.

Terminology

Census: An official count of all people living in a country or particular area.

Enumeration: The process by which people are counted for a census.

Enumeration District: The geographic area assigned to an enumerator.

Enumerator: Census taker.

Federal Census: A decennial census mandated and performed by the United States federal government beginning in 1790.

Non-Population Schedule: Enumerations in addition to the decennial population schedule providing information about a variety of subjects including agriculture, social statistics, industry and manufacturing, and more. These are also called supplemental schedules or special schedules.

Population Schedule: An enumeration of the population taken every ten years to determine needs in education, housing, and more. The information collected varies by year.

Schedule: A completed census worksheet.

Slave Schedule: Separate census schedules were used in 1850 and 1860 to enumerate enslaved individuals. Unfortunately, these are listed by name of slave owner and many are not indexed.

State Census: A census taken by mandate of individual state governments. A state census usually occurs between federal census years.

Source Citations

W hile most of today's software will guide us through the process, it is still important to understand the basic parts of a proper source citation when conducting your research. This citation is your proof positive of the record for others who view your research. It is also your breadcrumb should you need to revisit it.

Below you'll find several examples of proper source citations for you to use. Take care with your citations, and always include them with your work.

Online Digital Image:

1920 US Federal Census, Turner County, Georgia, population schedule, Amboy, enumeration district (ED) 140, supervisor's district (SD) 3, sheet 3B, dwelling 55, family 55, James T. Bullington household; digital image, Ancestry.com (http://www.ancestry.com : downloaded 18 February 2012); National Archives microfilm publication T625 roll 282.

Index Entry:

Carol Carnahan, "1850 US Federal Census," index, USGenWeb Free Census Project, Ohio Online Inventory (http://usgwcensus.org/cenfiles/oh/ashtabula/1850/pg0167b.txt : accessed 30 December 2012), entry for Abigail Chapman (age 50), Ashtabula County, Ohio, population schedule; sheet 167B, household 1, family 1. National Archives microfilm publication M452, roll 659.

Non-Population Schedule:

1870 US Census, Mahaska County, Iowa, "Mortality Schedule," Schedule 2, Madison Township, sheet 634, Joshua Crispin; NARA microfilm publication T1156, roll 57.

State Census:

1865 Iowa State Census, Poweshiek County, population schedule, Jackson township, page 26, dwelling 81, family 81, W.J. Lyons household; State Historical Society of Iowa, Iowa City, Iowa; ; microfilm IA_64.

Research Toolkit

USGenWeb Free Census Project

Research, learn, and get involved with this free census project through USGenWeb.

http://bit.ly/1NHVpfT

National Archives 1940 Census Records

The release of the 1940 census allows many of us to see our parents on a census for the first time. Learn what makes this census different.

http://1.usa.gov/1WL7l6y

National Archives: Census Records

Learn about the records held by NARA that can help you with your research.

http://1.usa.gov/1MUDtQw

Barb Snow's Your Guide to Finding and Using U.S. Census Records

This link-heavy article will get you well on your way through your research.

http://bit.ly/20KsFZf

Census Finder

Find links to census records, transcriptions, questions, and more for the United States Federal Census as well as those from select countries.

http://bit.ly/1WL7y9M

Steve Morse: One Step US Census 1790-1940

Scroll down approximately one-third of the way down the page for a list of Steve Morse's best links for census research.

http://bit.ly/1M4csq7

US Census Bureau

Grab information from the source!

http://1.usa.gov/1M4csX6

Cyndi's List: US Census Records

As always, Cyndi provides an extensive list of census-related links.

http://bit.ly/1SgadSf

FamilySearch Wiki: United States Census

Find links to articles and records sets accessible on line for free through FamilySearch.

http://bit.ly/1MmpahO

The Source: Overview of the US Census

An overview provided by the Ancestry Wiki.

http://ancstry.me/1kKgCu0

Red Book: Locate US Census records by state

Use this extensive guide to find out where the records you need are located.

http://ancstry.me/1MJg2mJ

Free Research Courses from FamilySearch

More than 40+ are for Census Research as well as other genealogy-related topics.

http://bit.ly/1MydD2I

Allen County Public Library Genealogy Center – Census Guide

This on line census guide is extremely helpful for getting up to speed.

http://bit.ly/1HFAELB

University of Virginia Library's Historical Census Browser

Interested in putting your ancestor into perspective? This browser will let you see the statistical data for a state or county by census year via chart or color map.

http://bit.ly/1Y2yr6b

Publications by the U.S. Census Bureau

This site lists publications pertaining to many contemporary and historical census years. Use the drop down menu to choose years related to your search.

http://1.usa.gov/1Pn2BQ2

Blank US Census Forms

Print blank census forms for your research. Free!

http://ancstry.me/1MUEsjs

FamilySearch Wiki: Soundex

Learn how this phonetic guide could help you with your search.

http://bit.ly/1Myei4a

Further Reading

Greenwood, Val D. *The Researcher's Guide to American Genealogy*. Third edition. Baltimore: Genealogical Publishing Co., 2000.

Hinckley, Kathleen W. *Your Guide to the Federal Census*. Cincinnati: Betterway Books, 2002.

Lainhart, Ann S. *State Census Records*. Baltimore: Genealogical Publishing Co., 1992.

Sperry, Kip, *Reading Early American Handwriting.* Baltimore: Genealogical Publishing Co., 2008.

Szucs, Loretto Dennis and Matthew Wright. *Finding Answers in U.S. Census Records.* Orem: Ancestry Publishing, 2002.

Thorndale, William and William Dollarhide, *Map Guide to the U.S. Federal Censuses, 1790-1920.* Baltimore: Genealogical Publishing Co., 1995.

Thank You

Thank you for purchasing this Quick & Easy Guide for Genealogists pocket guide. I hope that it has been a helpful resource in your family history research. I'd love to hear from you. If you'd like to share your research stories or ask me about something in this guide, please email me at: **stephanie@stephaniefishman.com**.

Check Out My Fiction

In addition to writing non-fiction, I love creating characters and story lines that speak to the heart of the reader. I'd love for you to sample my stories for free.

Get a free copy of *Shutter Step*, a short fiction anthology by five indie authors, for free when you sign up at my website. Each story will take you someplace different - in five minutes or less. It's perfect for slipping time in with a book during your busy day.

Visit my website to get your free copy.

www.stephaniefishman.com/shutter-step

About the Author

I chase dead people. I've grown up hearing family stories all of my life. In 1998, I picked up a new hobby as a way to pass the time with my grandmother. I now perform genealogical research for clients as well. I love to discover and share the stories of our ancestors. The words found in documents like marriage records and newspaper articles tell the stories of our families. In addition to providing research services, I enjoy creating narratives of family stories for my relatives as well as the relatives of clients. I am also active as a presenter speaking to genealogy groups and societies on topics related to family history research.

I've been a freelance writer for several years writing mostly on the subject of family history for blogs, websites, and genealogy societies and publications. I've also been a ghostwriter for areas ranging from air conditioning to the food service industry. I've enjoyed writing about family history much more than Chinese food. I'm a 14-year veteran homeschool mom who tries her best to raise creative and curious kids. Two have survived into adulthood, so we can't be all that bad at it. The youngest is a triple threat: writer, musician, and artist. I'm hoping to work on a few projects with her in the future.

My favorite book will always be Rebecca by Daphne DuMaurier. I remember sitting in the classroom after school as my eighth grade English teacher introduced me to it. I had read everything on our list for that grade so she gave me her favorite titles to read instead. I also learned that at age thirteen I didn't enjoy Steinbeck but I loved Orwell.

During high school and college I bounced between creative and nonfiction writing with even a stint on a community college newspaper. I was just too nervous to tell anyone about it. Very few people read my words so it surprises me that my parents knew I wanted to be a writer before I was able to speak it aloud. As I got closer to a milestone year I decided to break out of my fear and start writing my books with the goal of sharing them with others. Finding Eliza, my first novel, was a fortieth birthday present to myself. I hope you've enjoyed it.

I'm in love with the Oxford Comma. I'm hopelessly addicted to having my heart ripped out by BBC dramas. I love to insert references to history, pop culture, and humor into my writing and conversation. I currently have purple hair. I believe Joss Whedon can strike creative lightning at whim.

Official Biography

Stephanie Pitcher Fishman is an author and professional genealogist specializing in Midwestern and Southeastern United States family history. In addition to the Quick & Easy Guide for Genealogists series, she is the author of four family history research guides in the Legacy QuickGuide series focusing on state-specific research techniques. She has also written articles and blog posts for websites such as Archives.com and is a co-founder of The In-Depth Genealogist. She also lectures on topics such as Plain Religions, Quaker research, and introducing family history to children. Ms. Fishman's first novel, *Finding Eliza*, was published in 2014. To learn more, visit: **www.StephanieFishman.com**.

Connect with Stephanie

Facebook

www.facebook.com/StephaniePitcherFishman

Facebook Group

www.facebook.com/groups/SPFforReaders

Twitter

@stephpfishman

Pinterest

www.pinterest.com/stephpfishman

Read More!

Finding Eliza

by Stephanie Pitcher Fishman

"It's just a little family history. What could go wrong?"

When Lizzie Clydell agreed to join her grandmother at the church's genealogy group meeting she expected nothing more than lemon squares and a few stories. Instead, an old diary leads

Lizzie down a dusty road of lies, hidden family secrets, and a lynching that nearly destroyed her family.

Still struggling with the loss of her parents two decades earlier, Lizzie must confront a painful past that others hoped was forgotten. Her journey becomes even more difficult as she realizes those around her may not be as they seem.

Reviews of Finding Eliza
by Other Readers

"Not since Steel Magnolias has a group of southern belles been as strong, charming, and funny. Throw in a compelling mystery and poignant history, and you've got a can't-put-down, can't-miss hit."

"Stephanie nailed this story from beginning to

end. Her writing sings and the story flows drawing you in and keeping you spellbound. I read straight through in less than 3 days because I simply couldn't put it down. I was lost in Lizzie's world of a young girl pushing back a deep hurt from years past, and her Grandmother and friends who loved her enough to help her face that hurt. Through the anguish experienced by her ancestors, who suffered through the deep darkness of a post-Civil War era, Lizzie comes to understand her own loss, and ultimately, to embrace it."

"What an amazing book! I can't imagine the emotions of finding out the history of one's past like this, and actually being there to see face the face the man responsible. I don't want to reveal too much in the review. But, please, read this book, it's amazing! It makes me want to dig into my family history."

"Finding Eliza by Stephanie Pitcher Fishman is a heartwarming book that pulled me in quite quickly. Fishman's love of genealogy and history is quite evident and she provides unvarnished glimpses of the not too distant past in the American South. I finished the book with two strong messages in mind: We have much to learn from history, especially our personal history and forgiveness has the power to set us free as long as we remember to forgive ourselves as well."

Finding Eliza

can be found on Kindle

and in paperback at

Amazon.com and Barnes & Noble.

Also by

Stephanie Pitcher Fishman

Fiction

Finding Eliza

Shutter Step

The Widow Teal: A serialized novel

Quick & Easy Guides For Genealogists

Researching Your Quaker Family History

Researching the Plain Religions

Research Bundle: Quakers & Plain Religions

Researching Your Ancestors Using the U.S. Census

Legacy Family Tree QuickGuides Series

Ohio Genealogy

Georgia Genealogy

Alabama Genealogy

Florida Genealogy

www.ingramcontent.com/pod-product-compliance
Lightning Source LLC
Chambersburg PA
CBHW071238280526
45787CB00002B/975